Sizzling Beach Babes

Hot Sexy Swimsuit Girls Models Pictures

By **PHOTO ART LOVER**

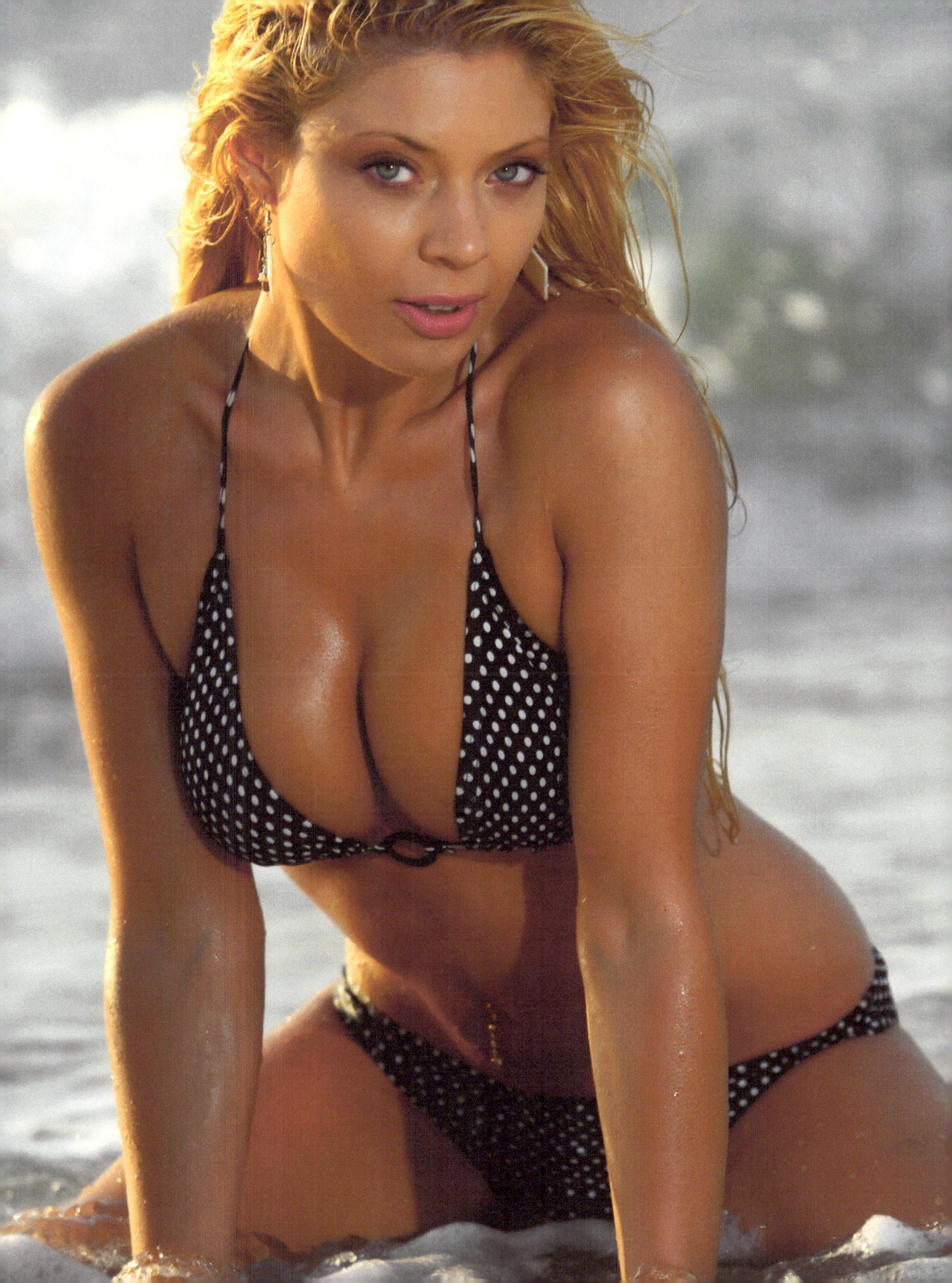

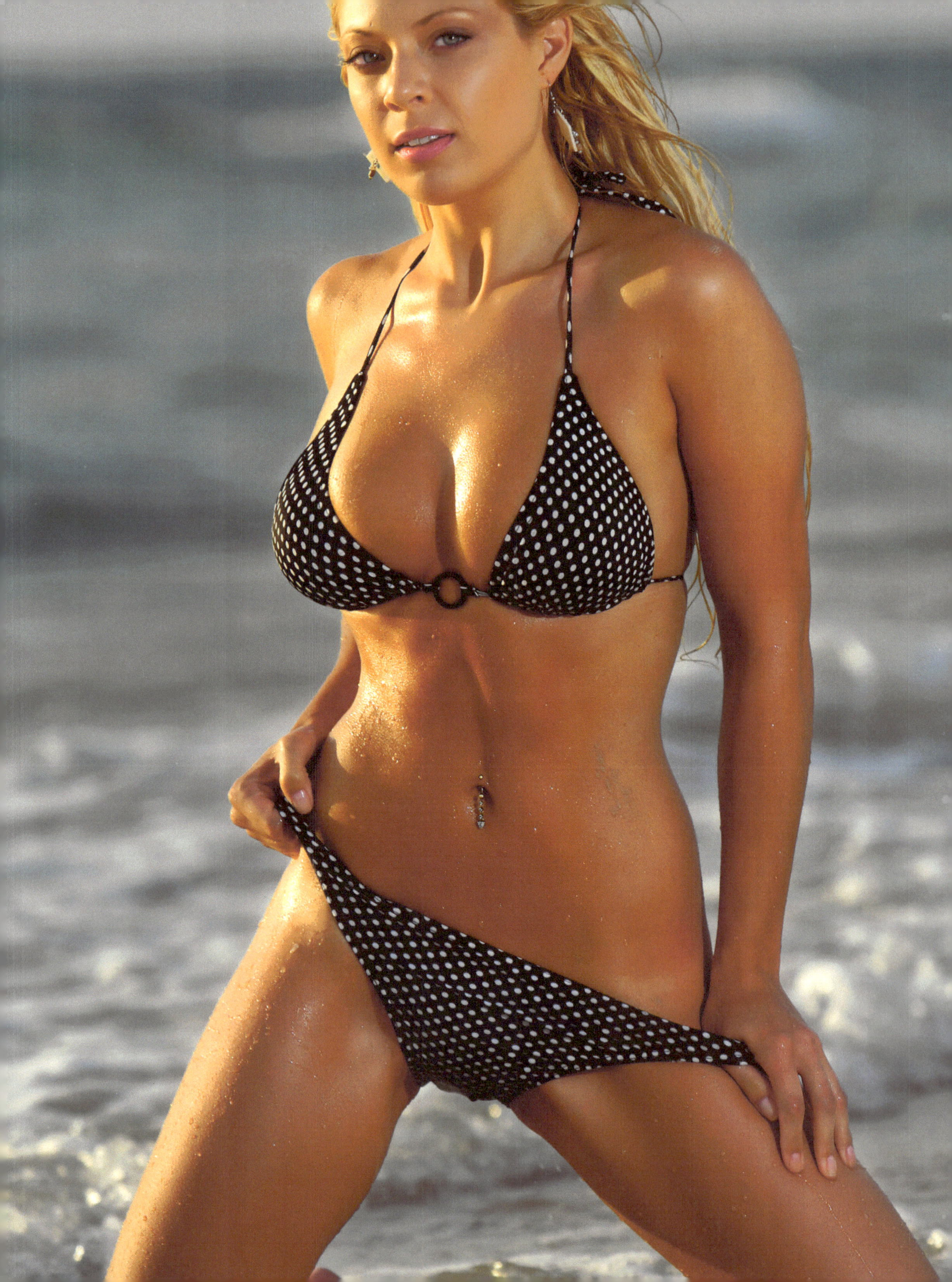

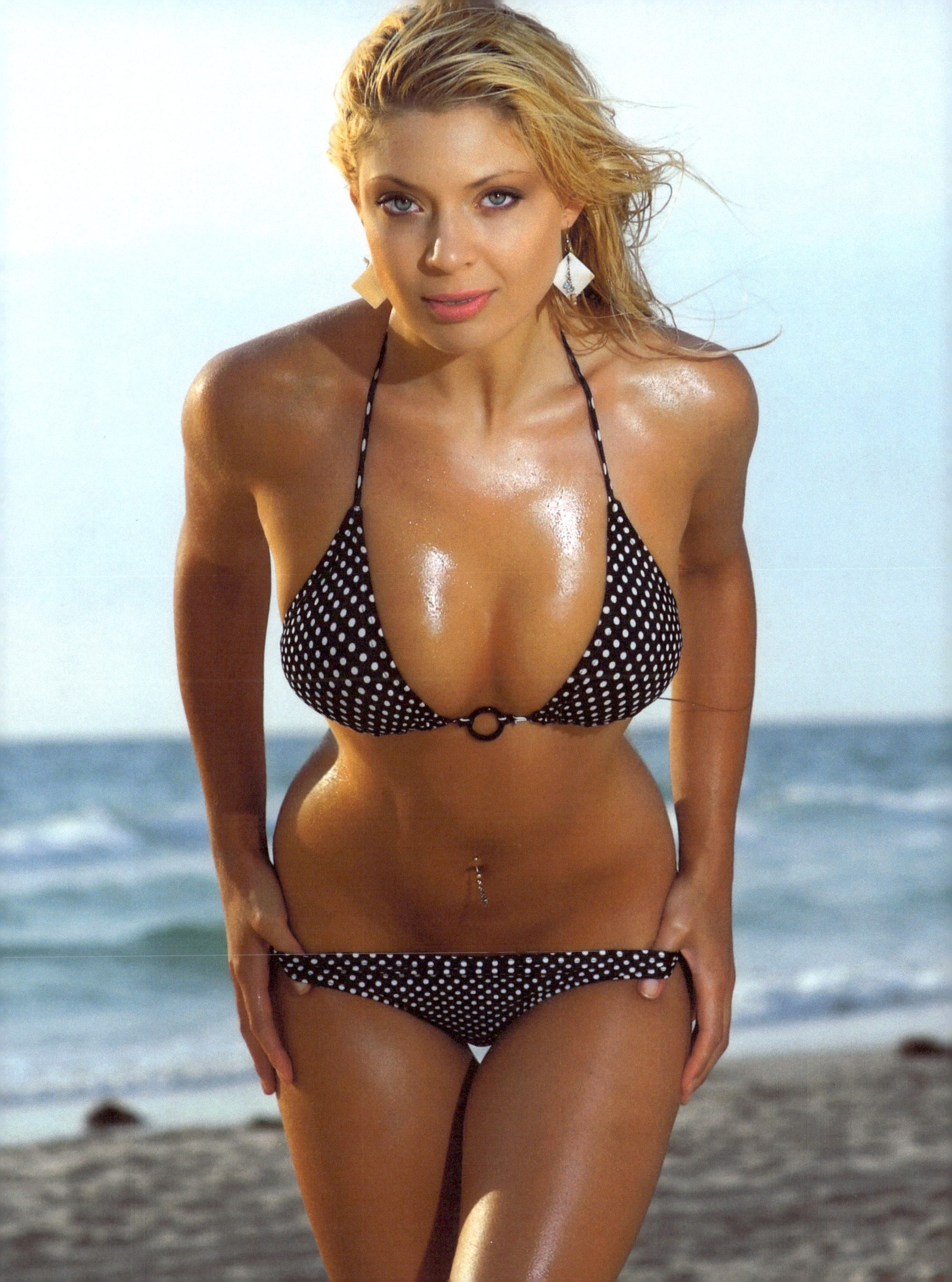

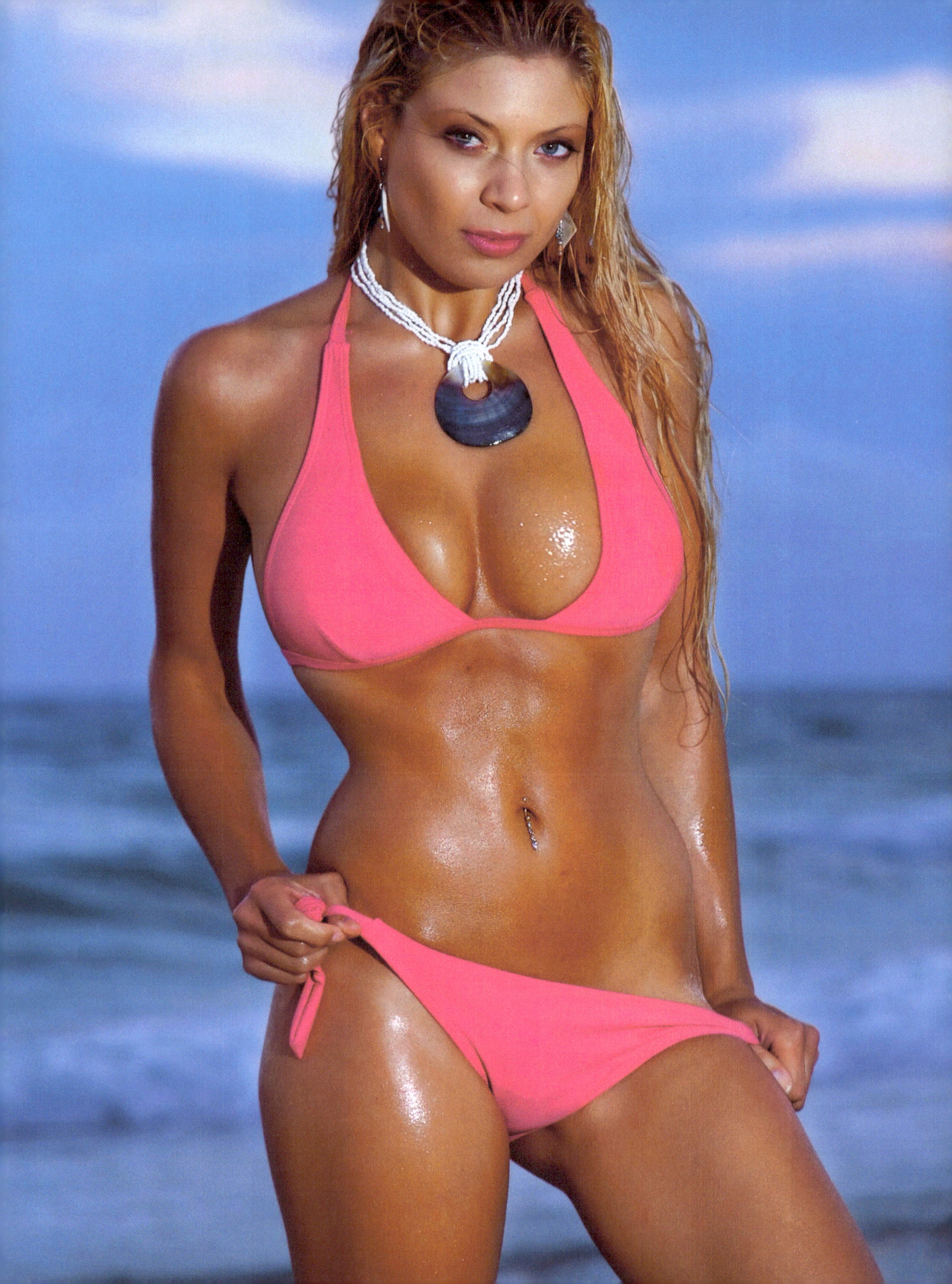

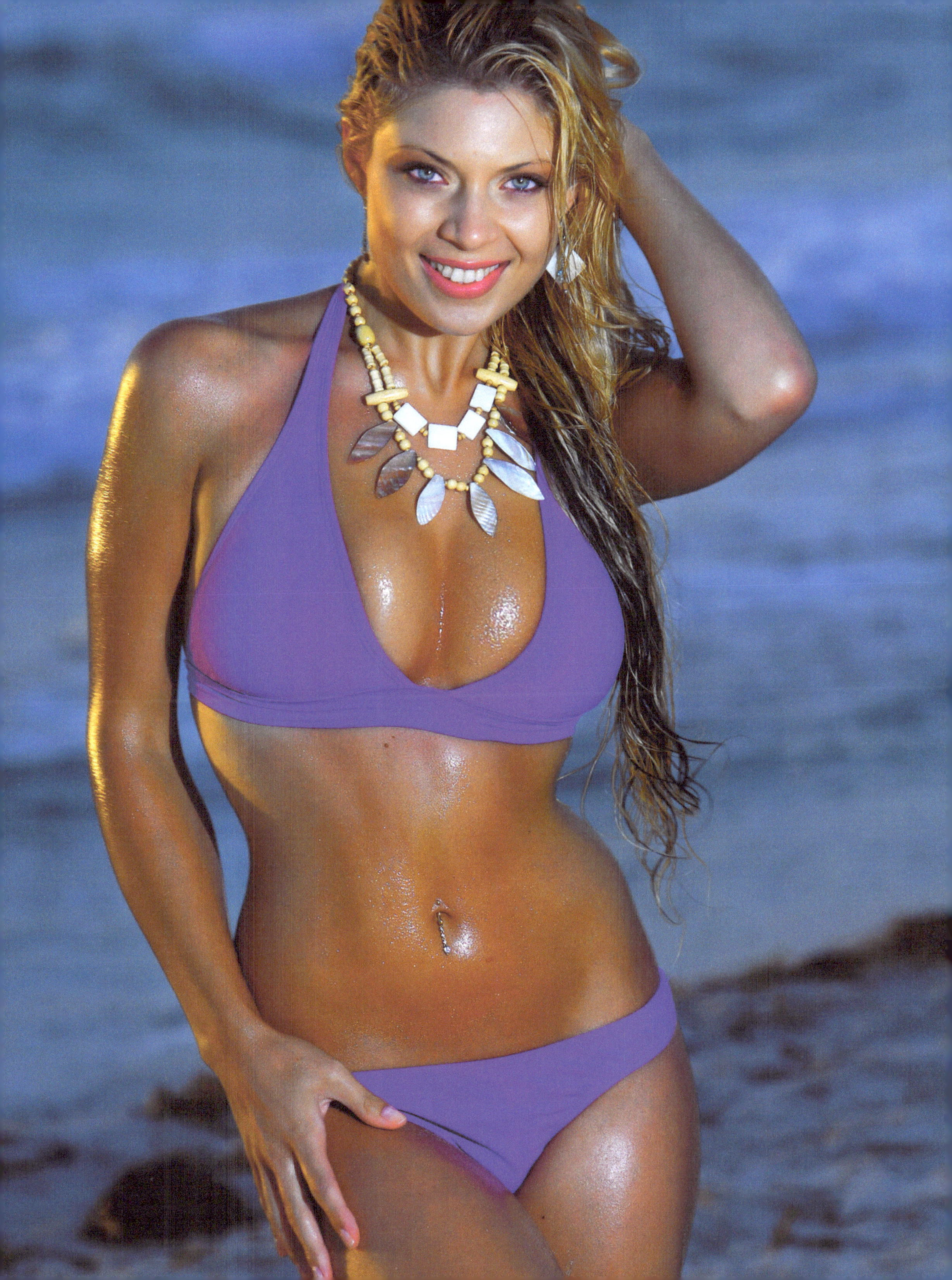

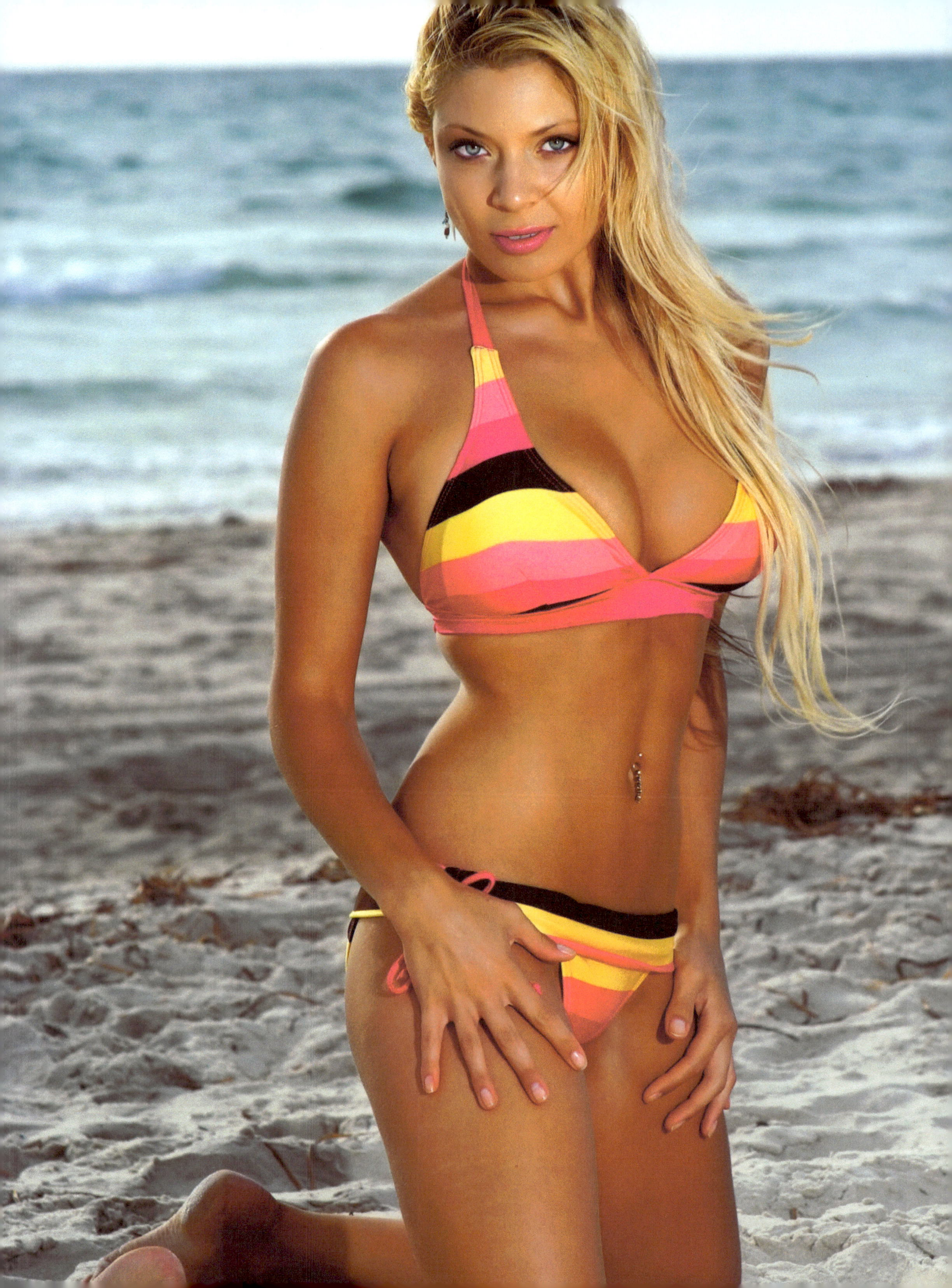

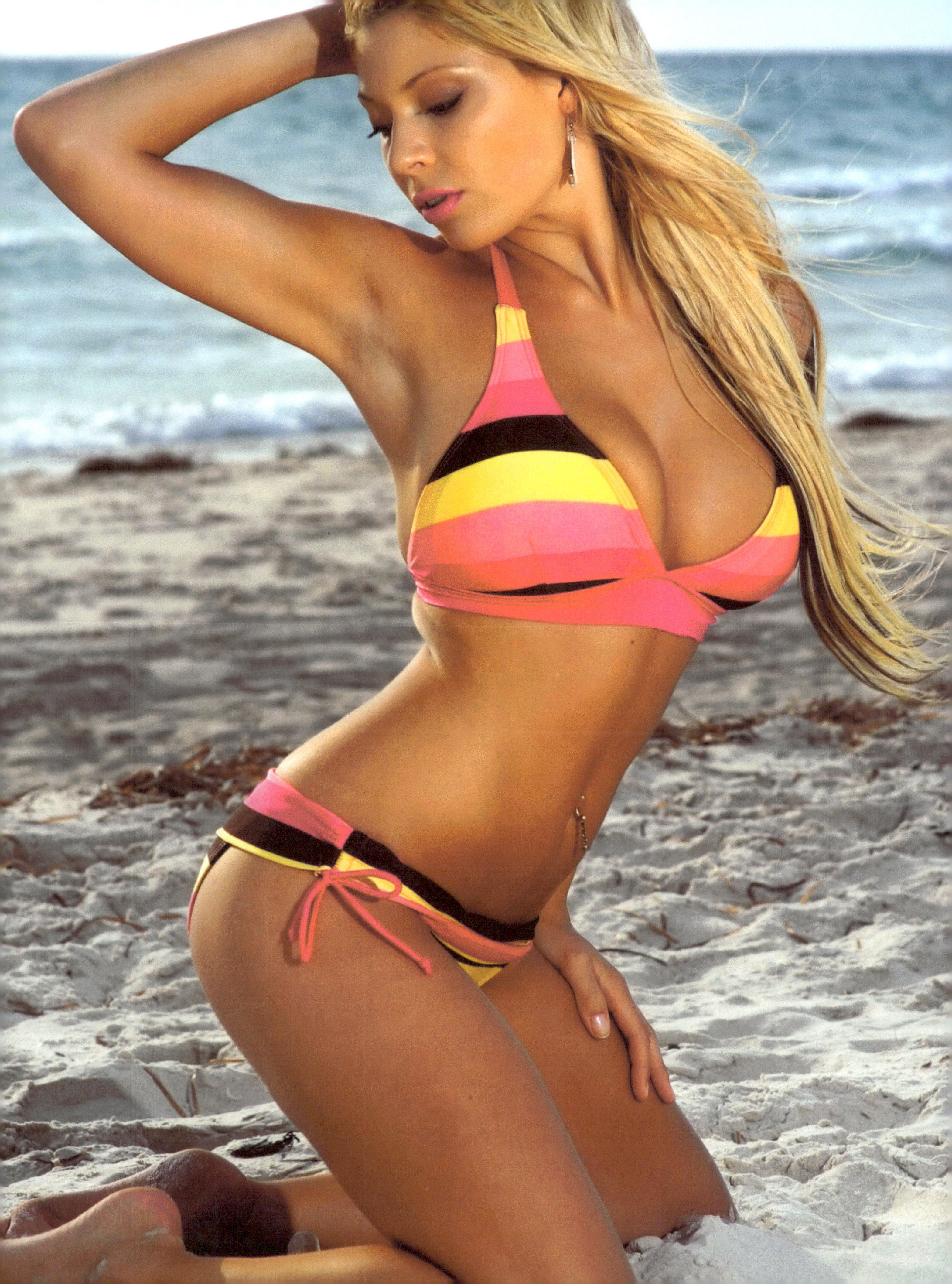

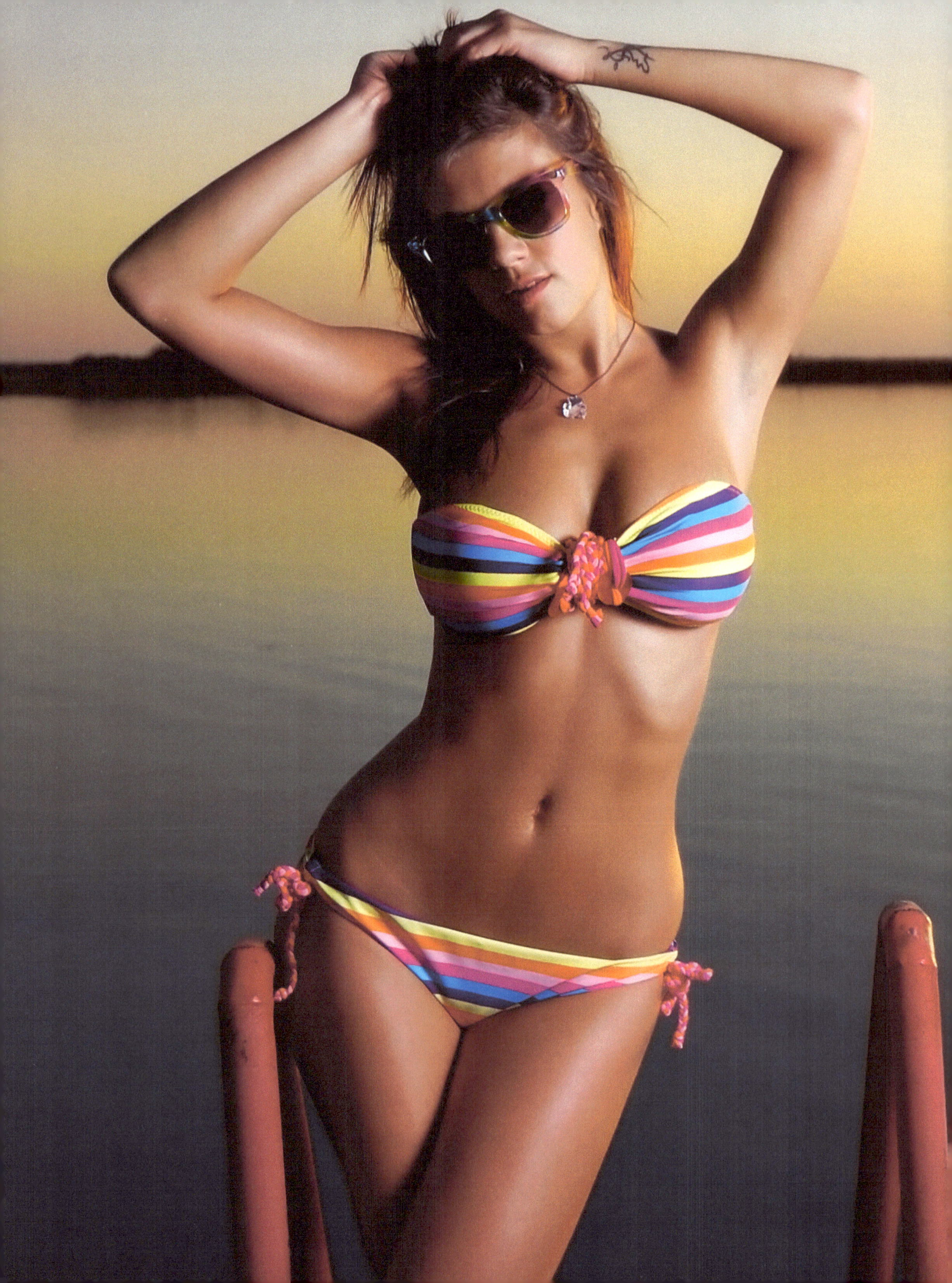

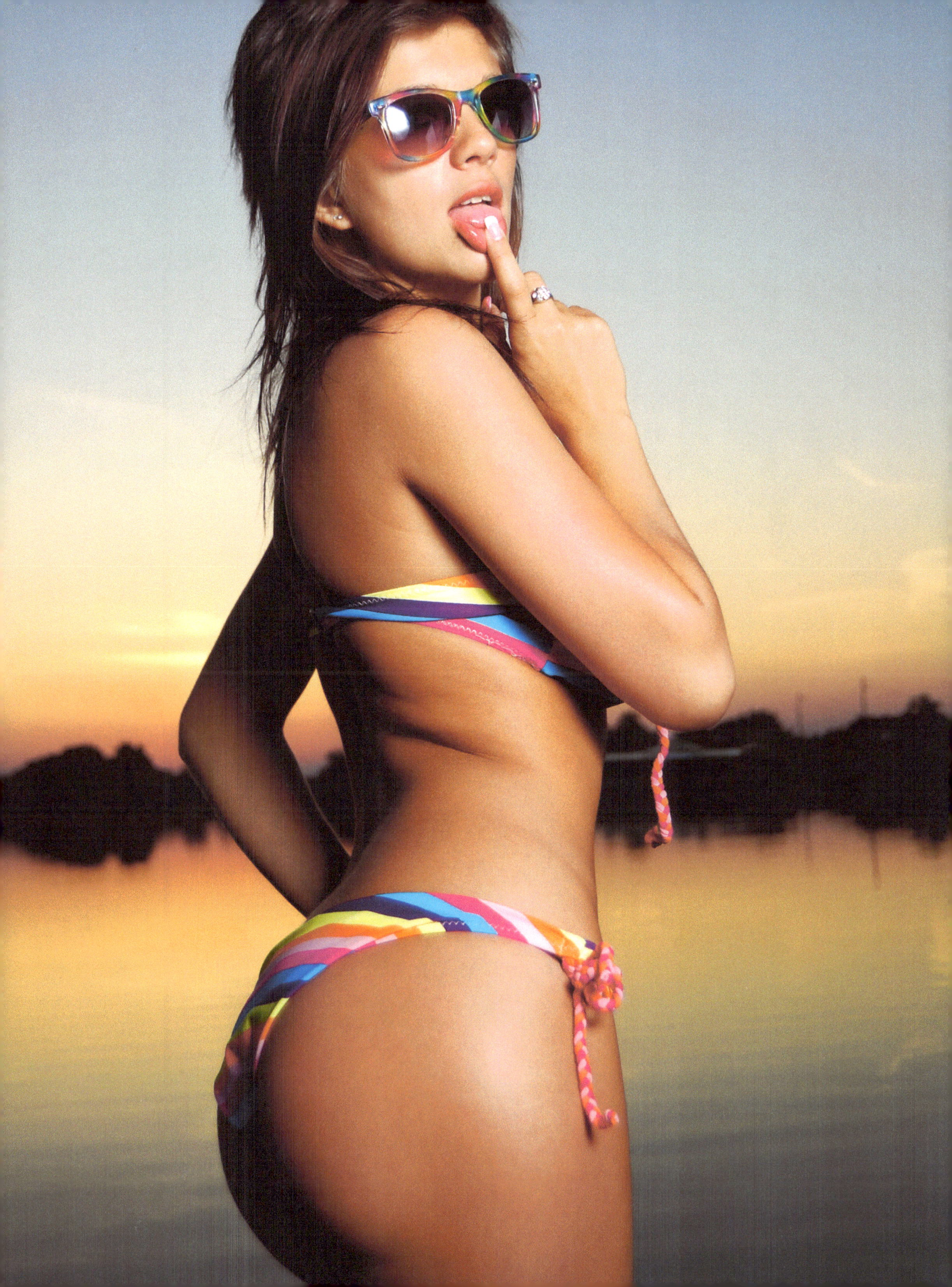

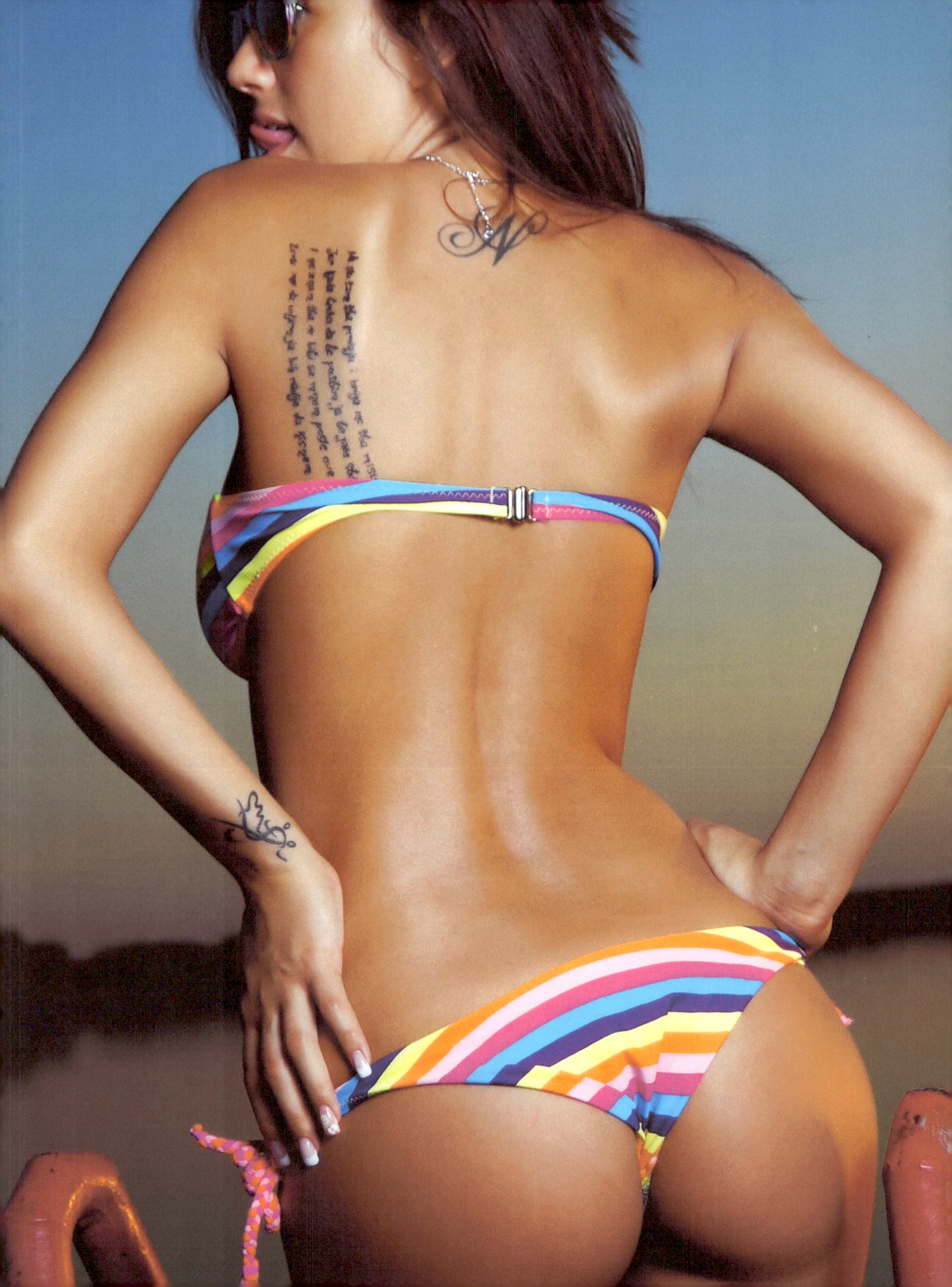

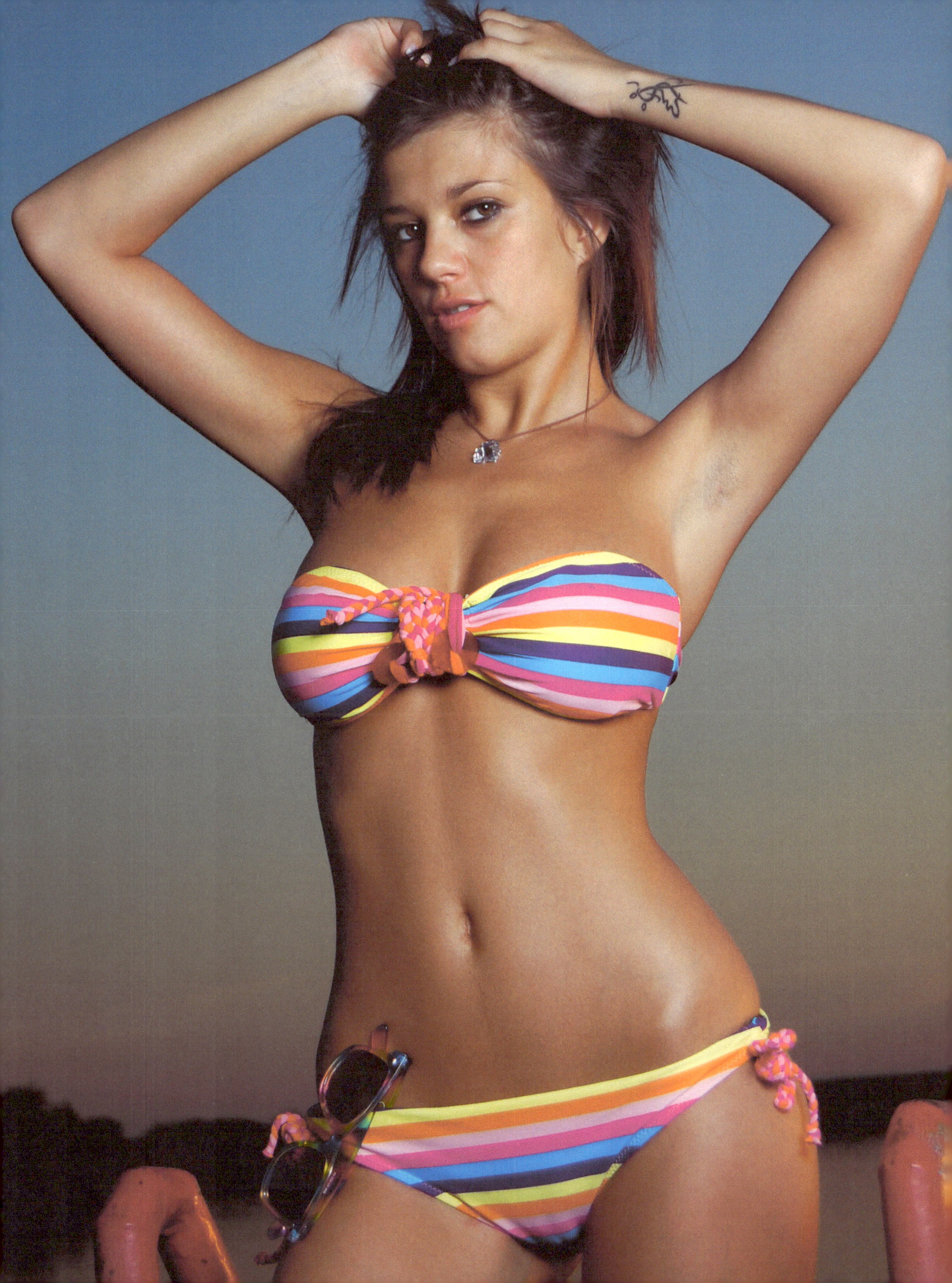

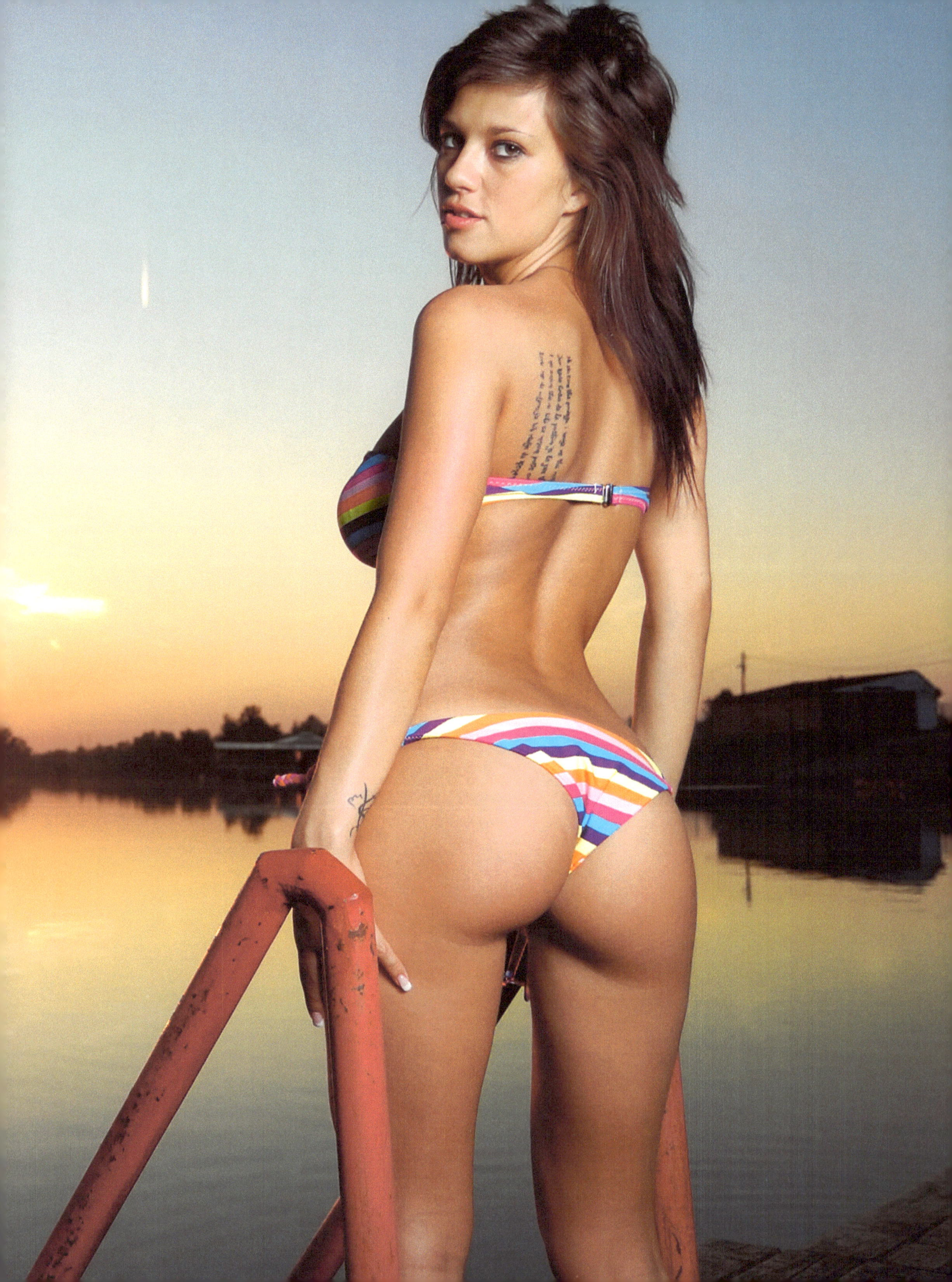

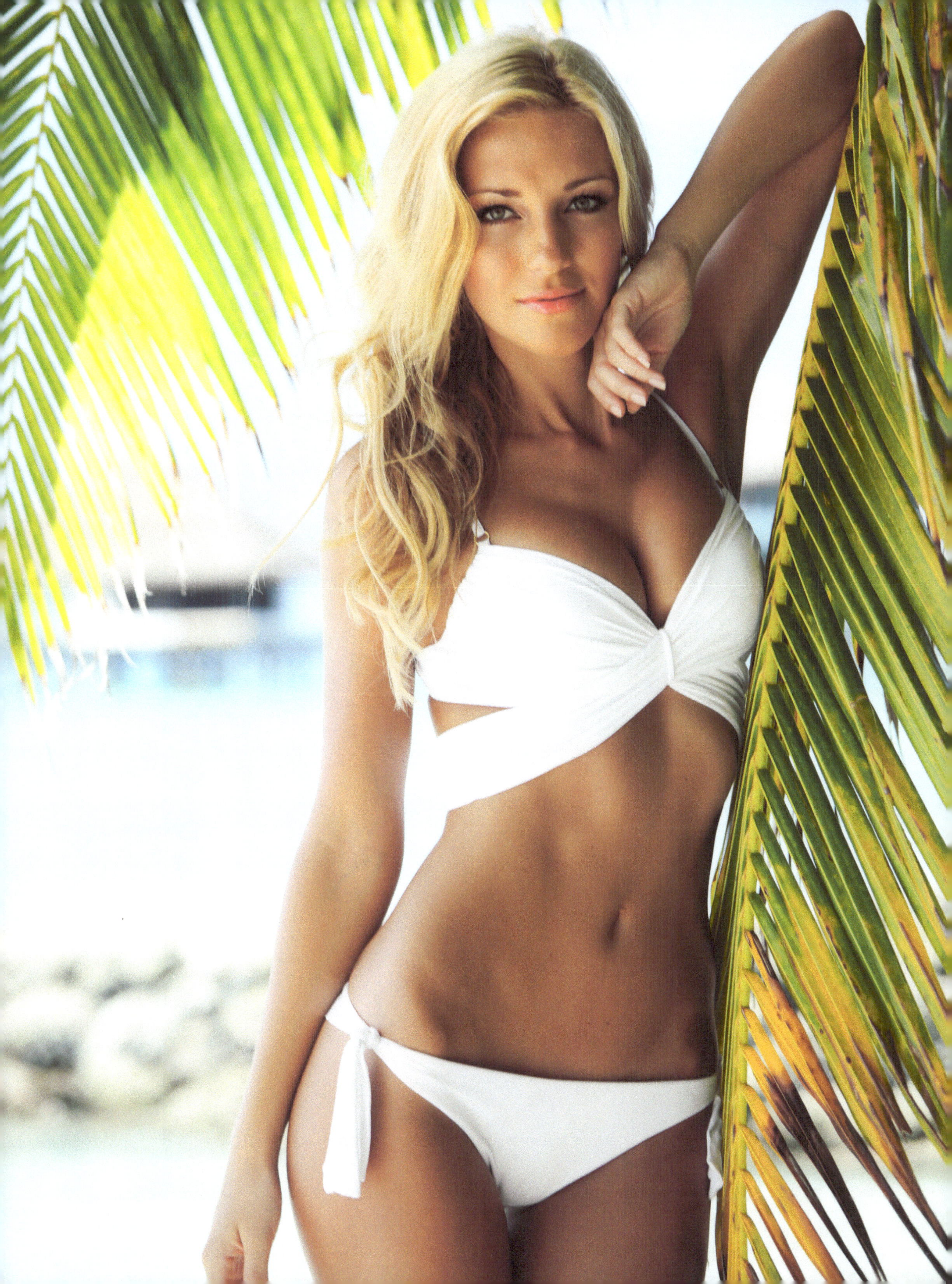

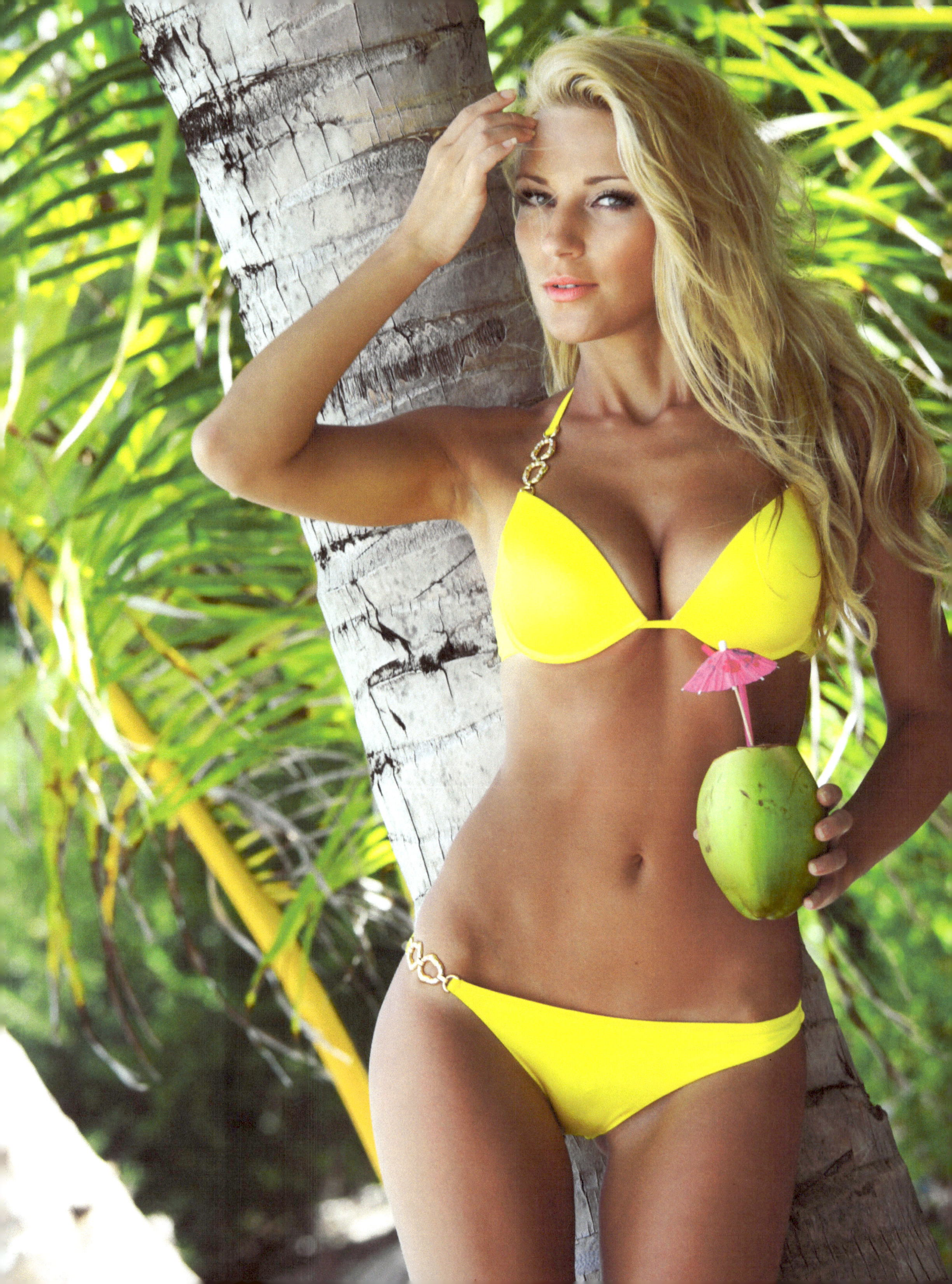

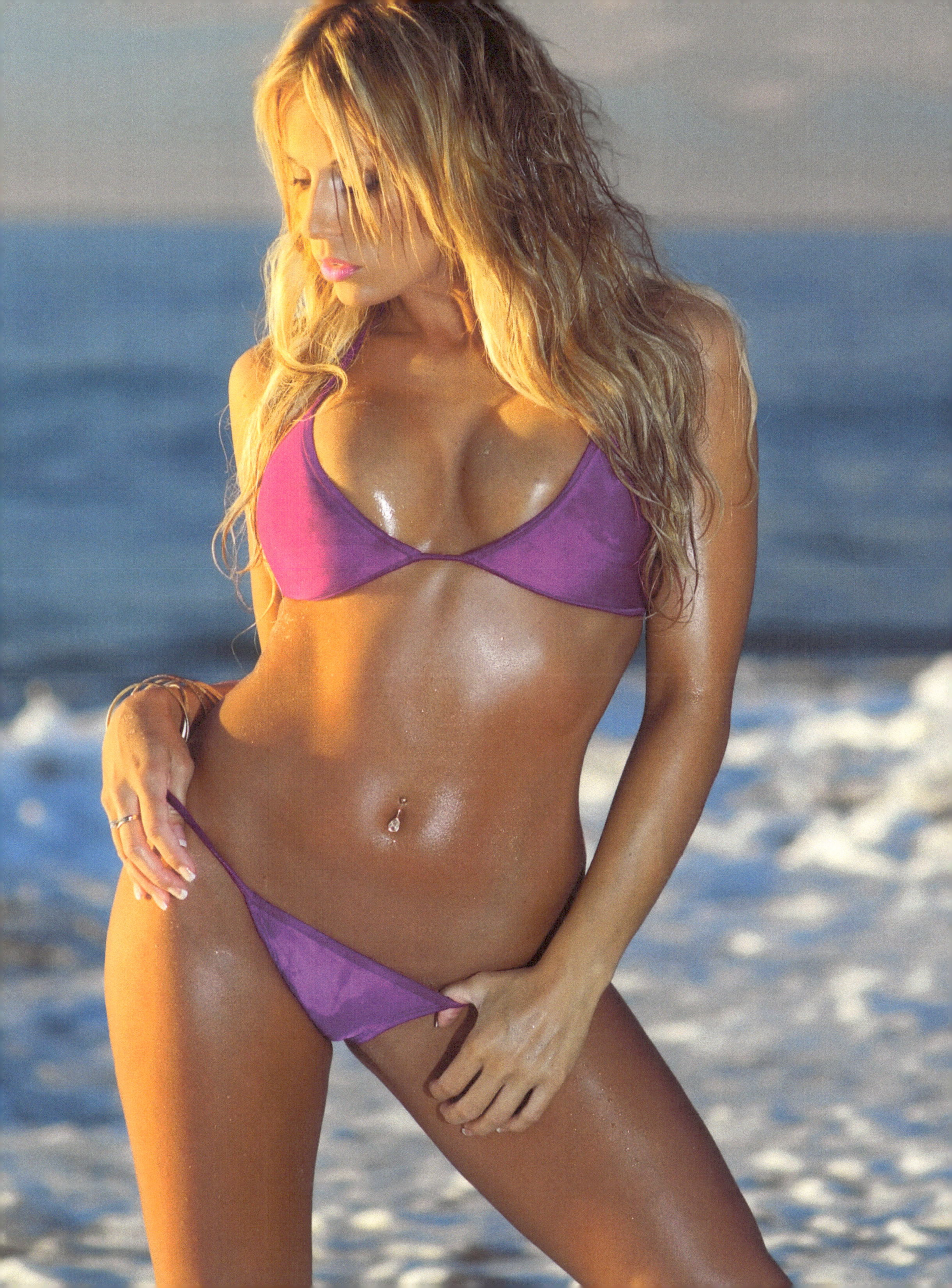

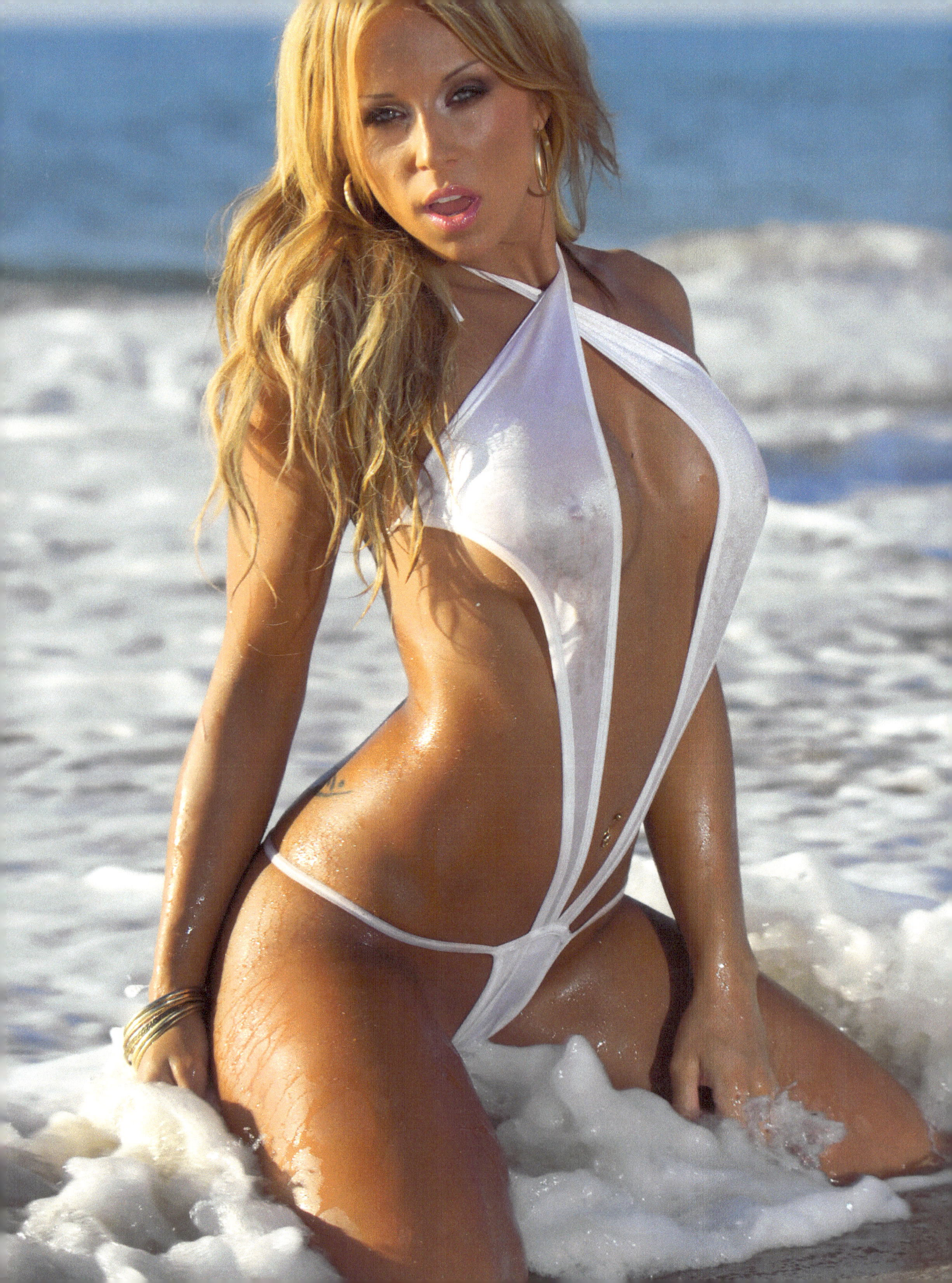

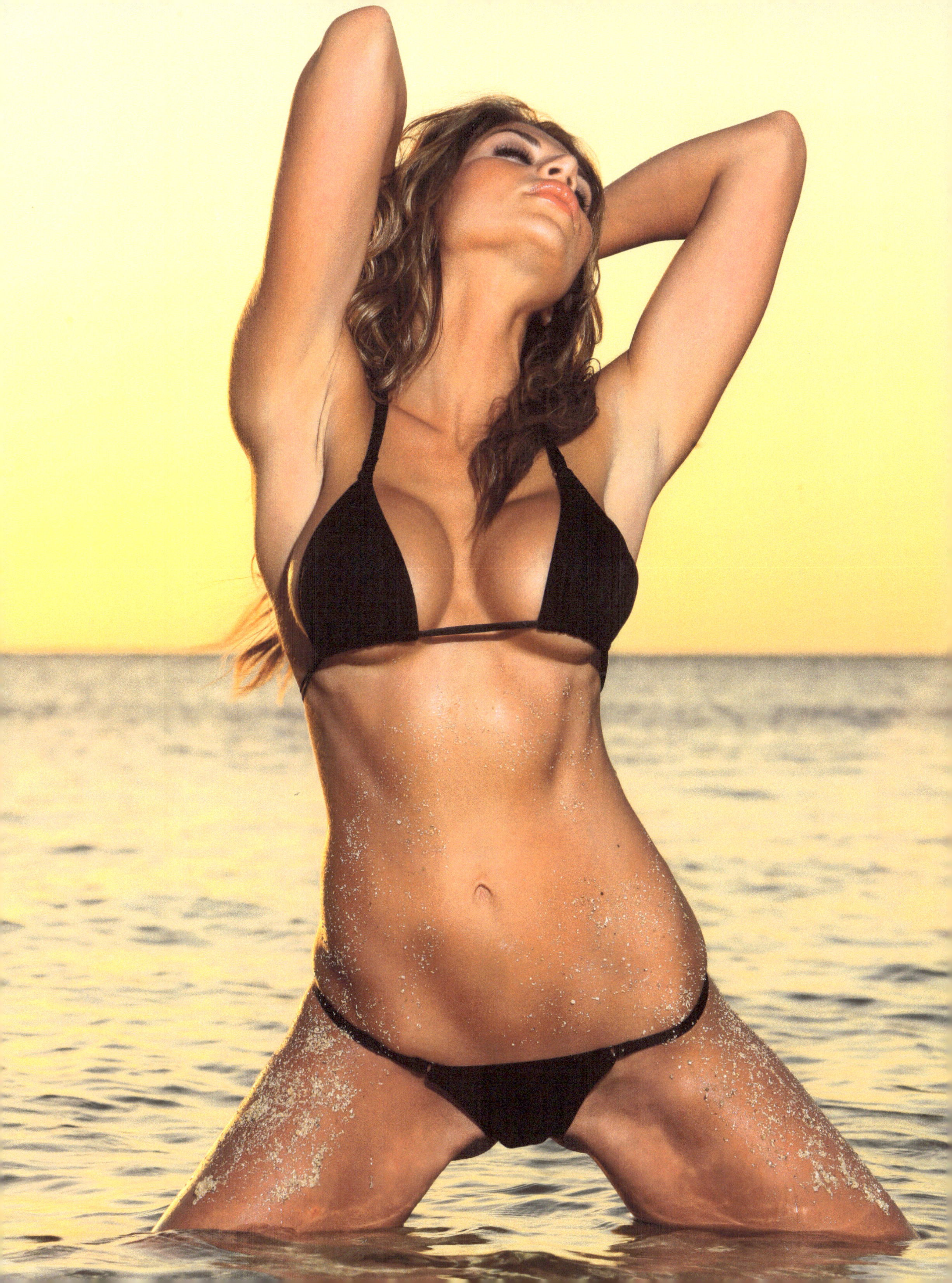

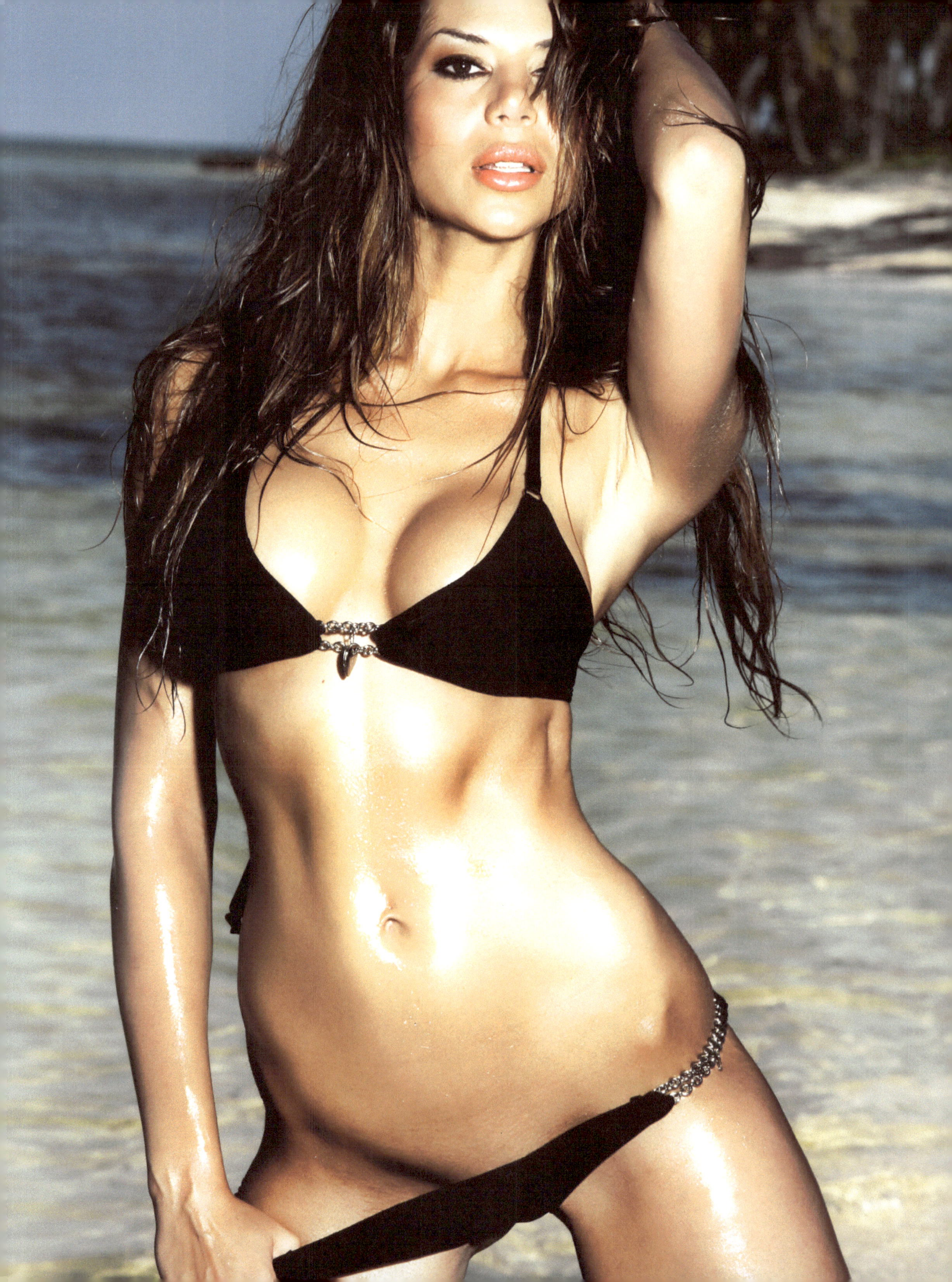

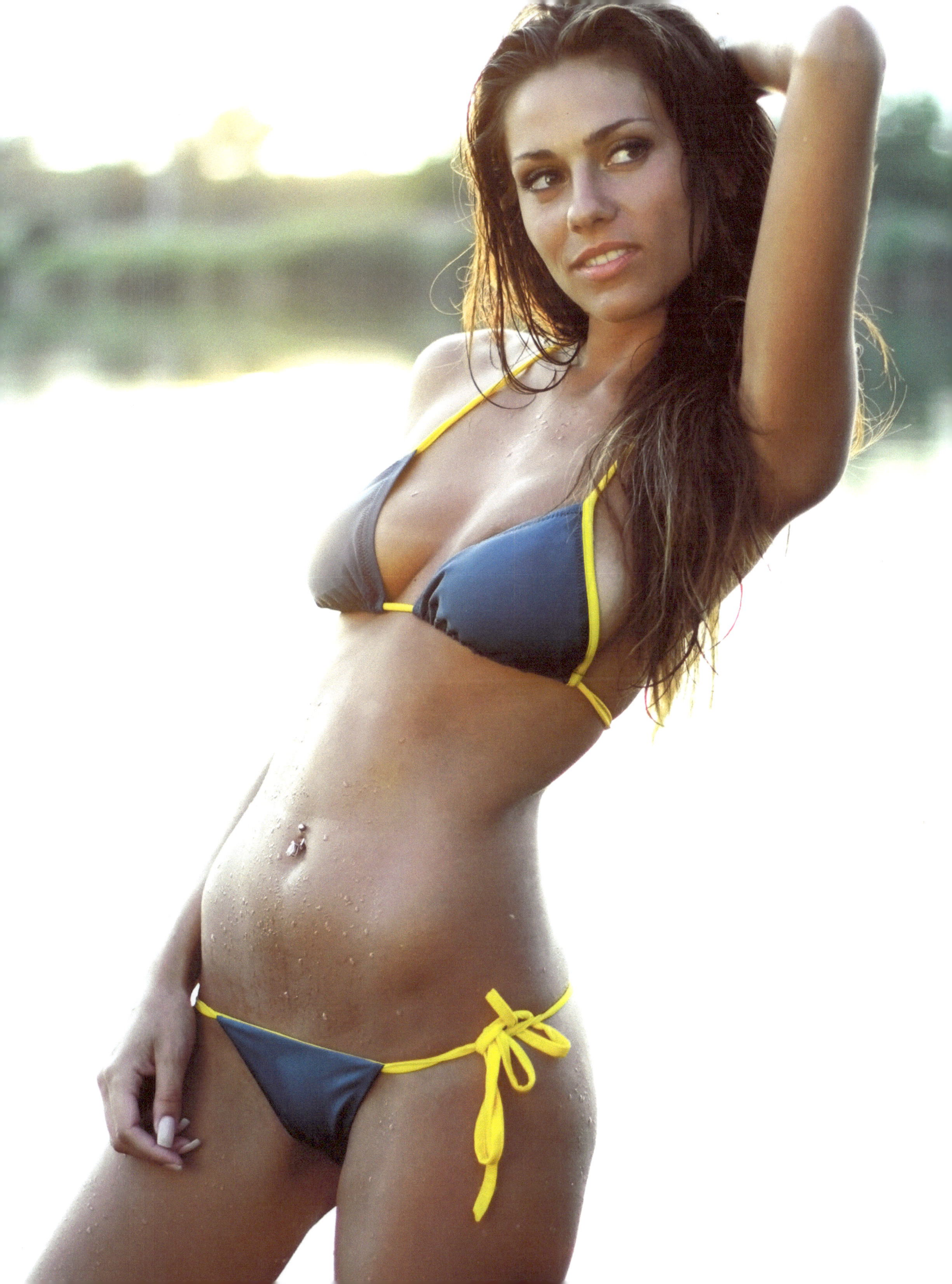

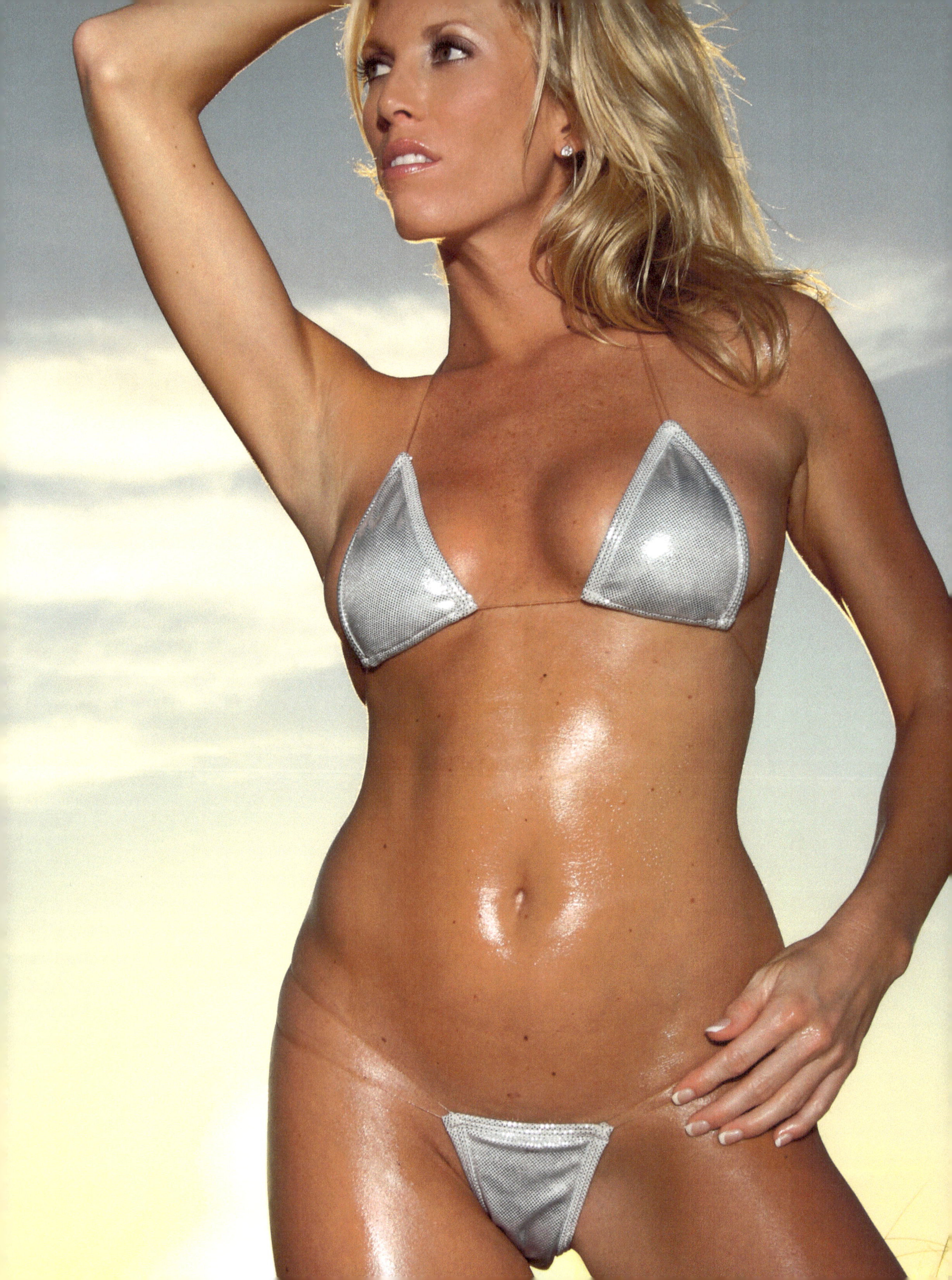

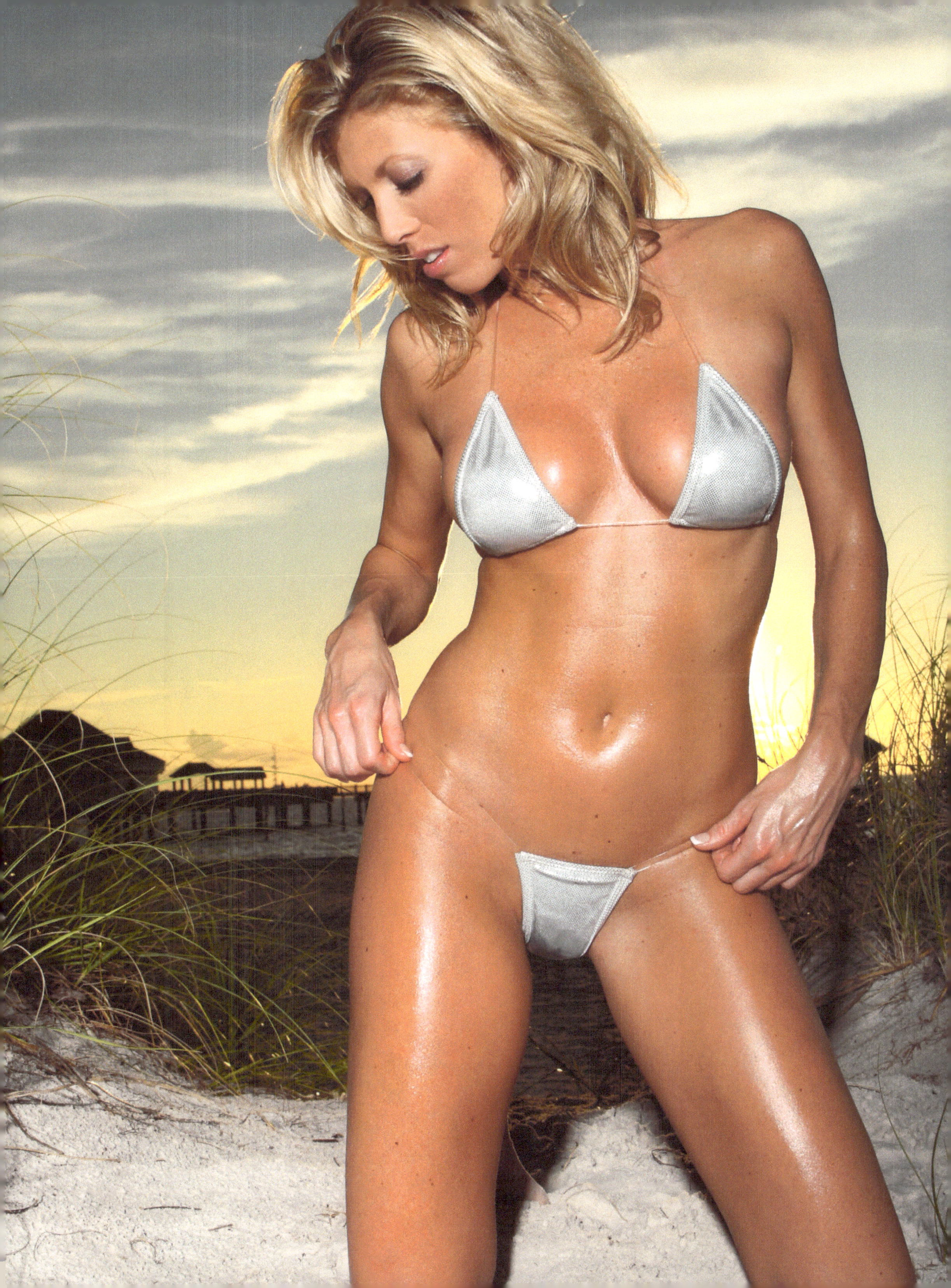

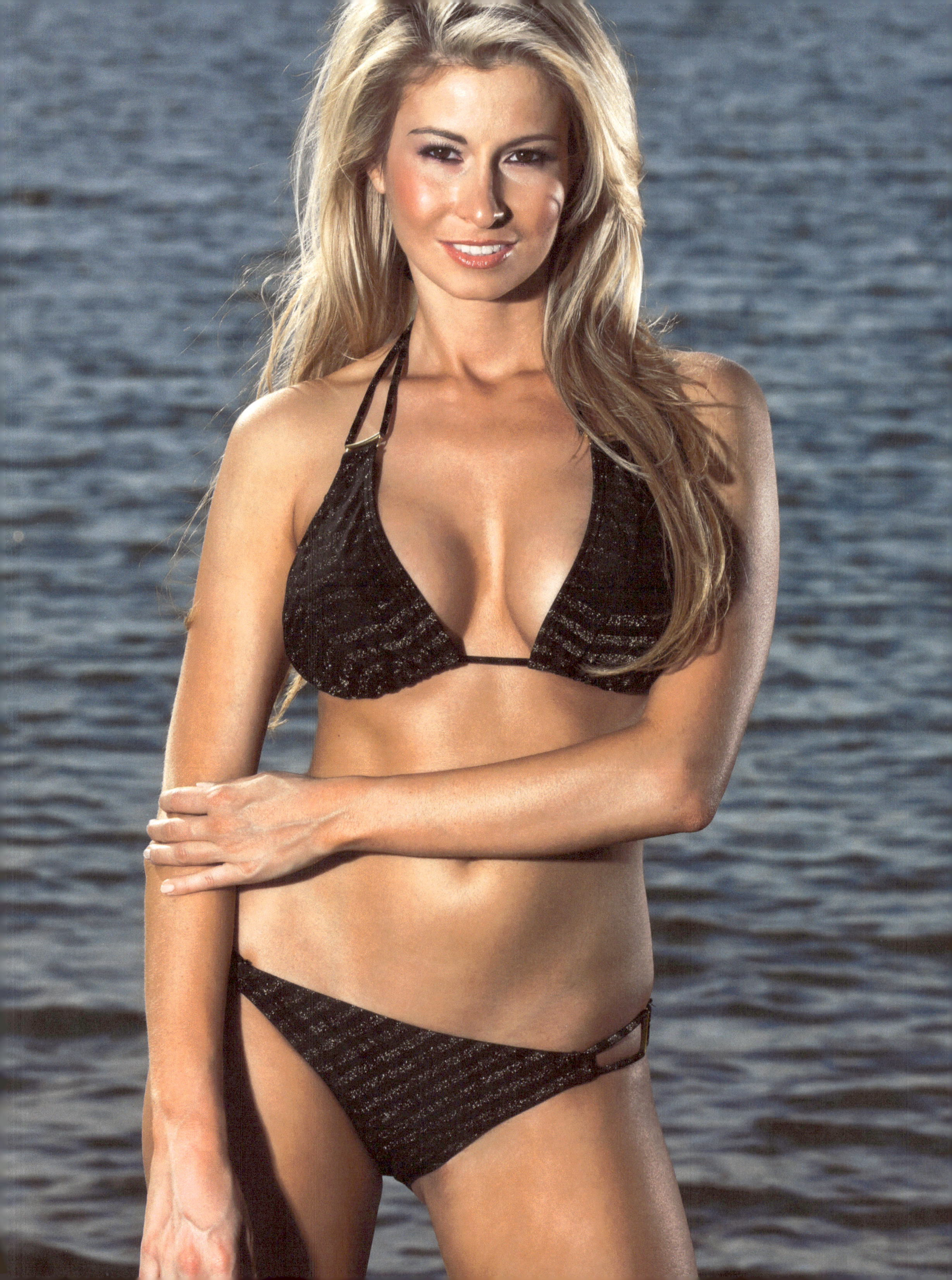

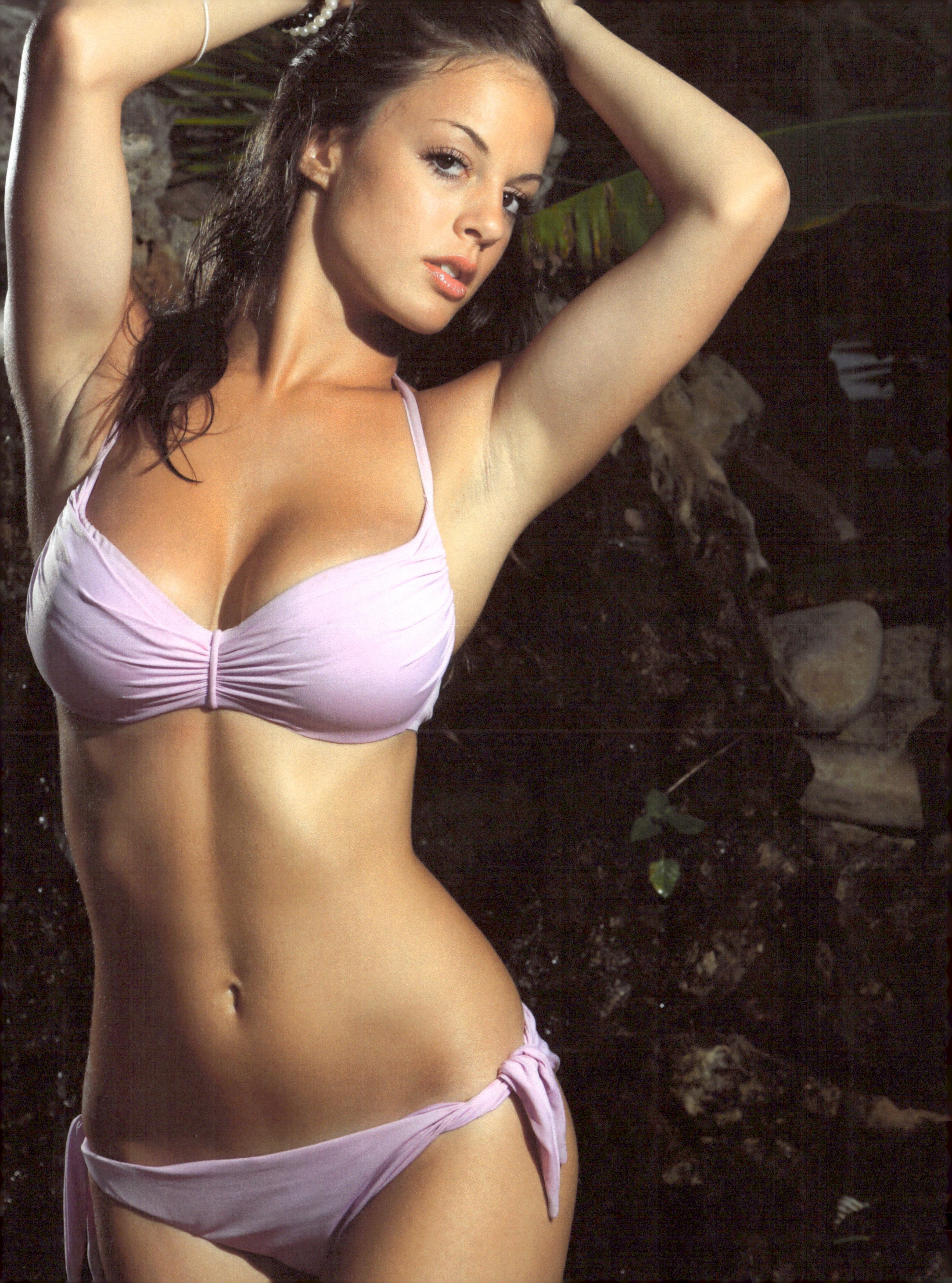

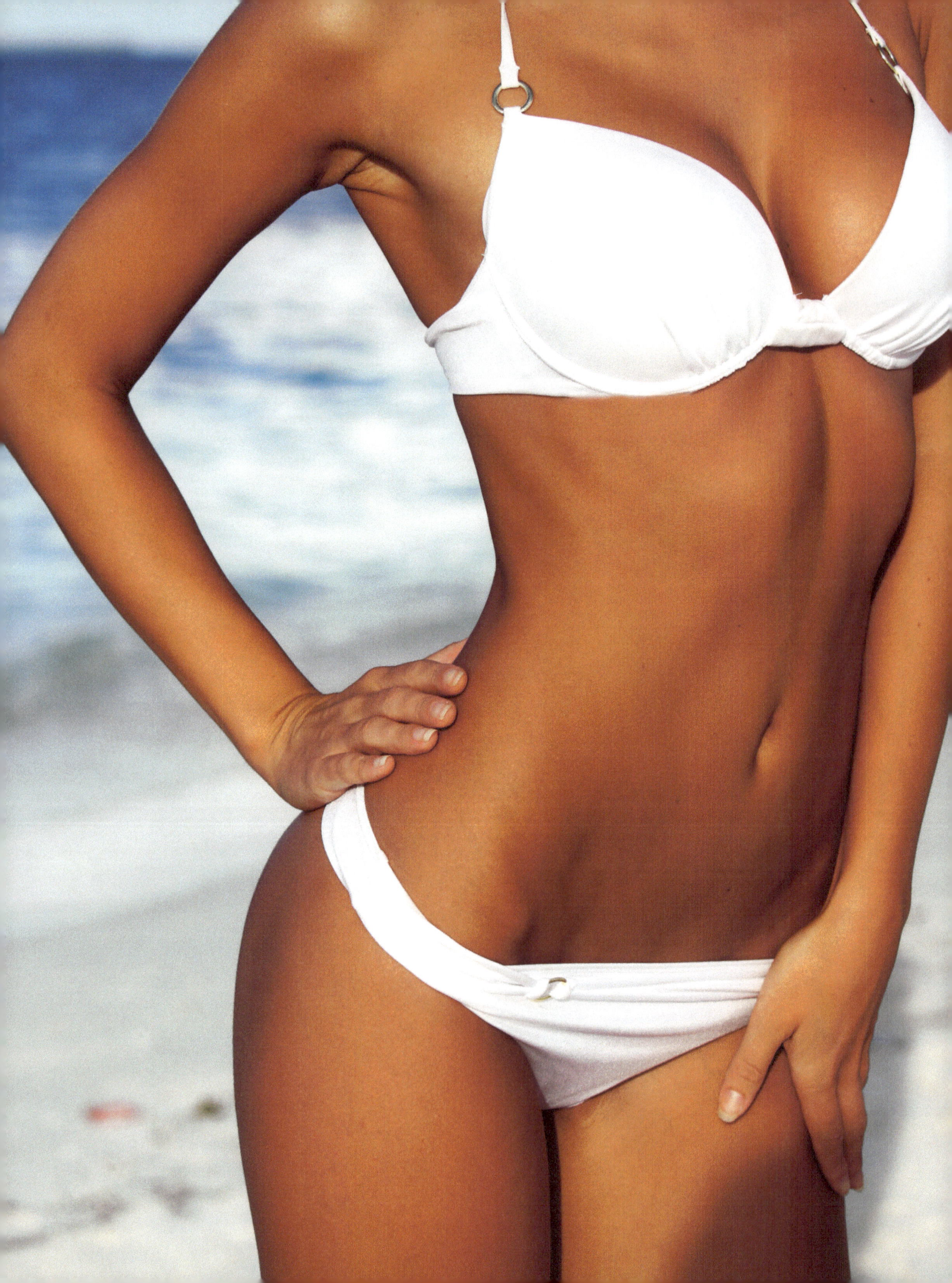

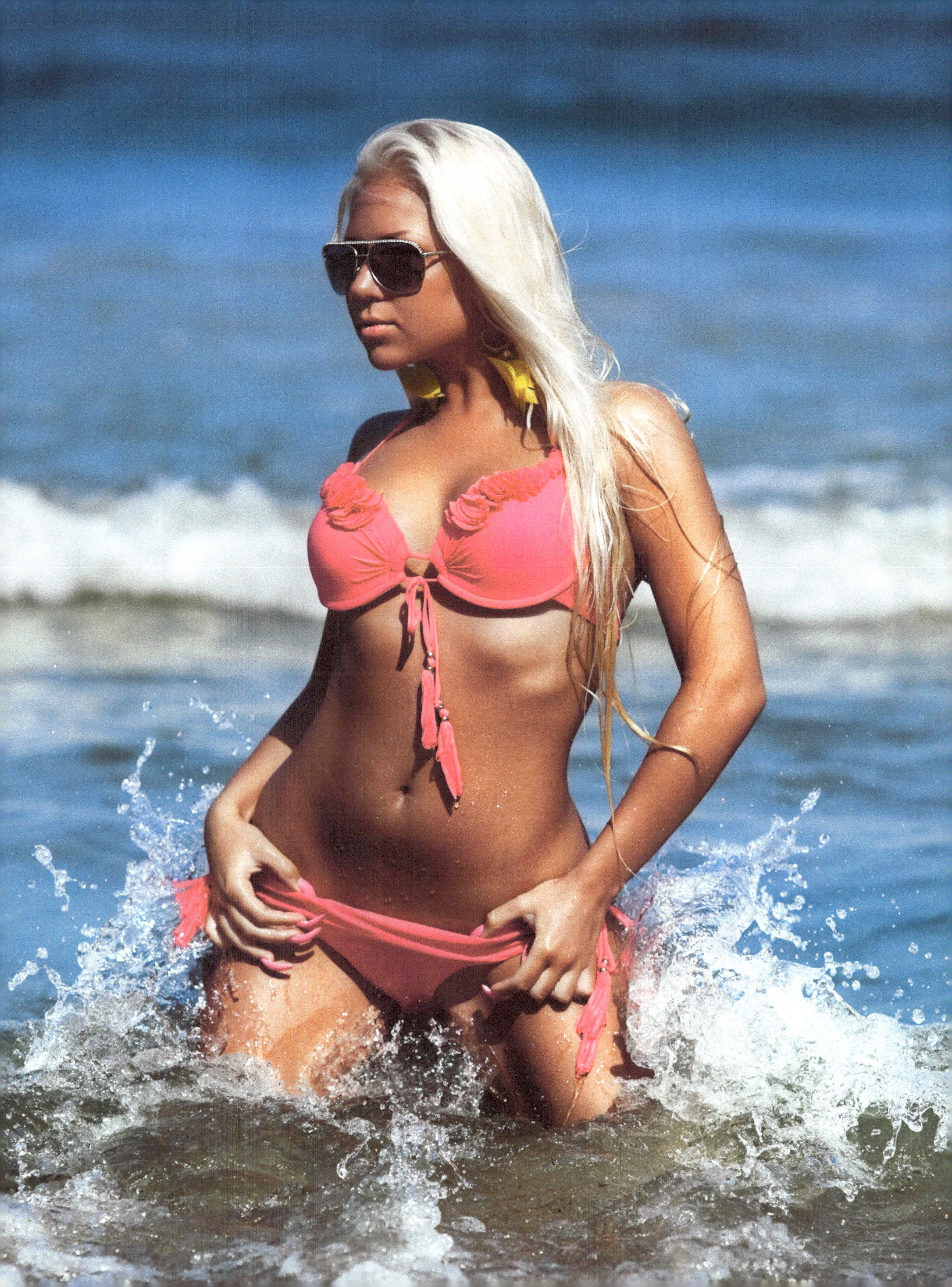

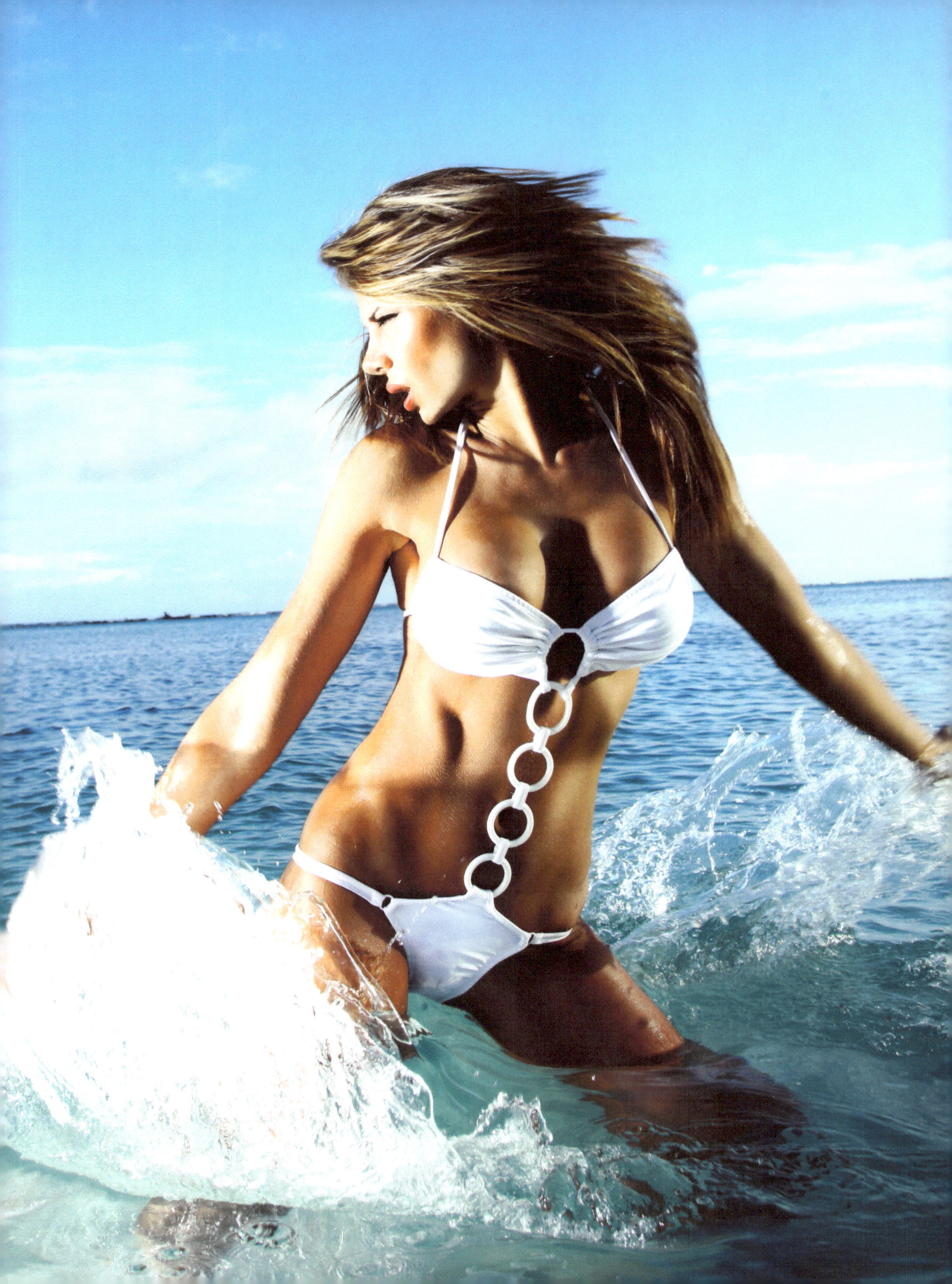

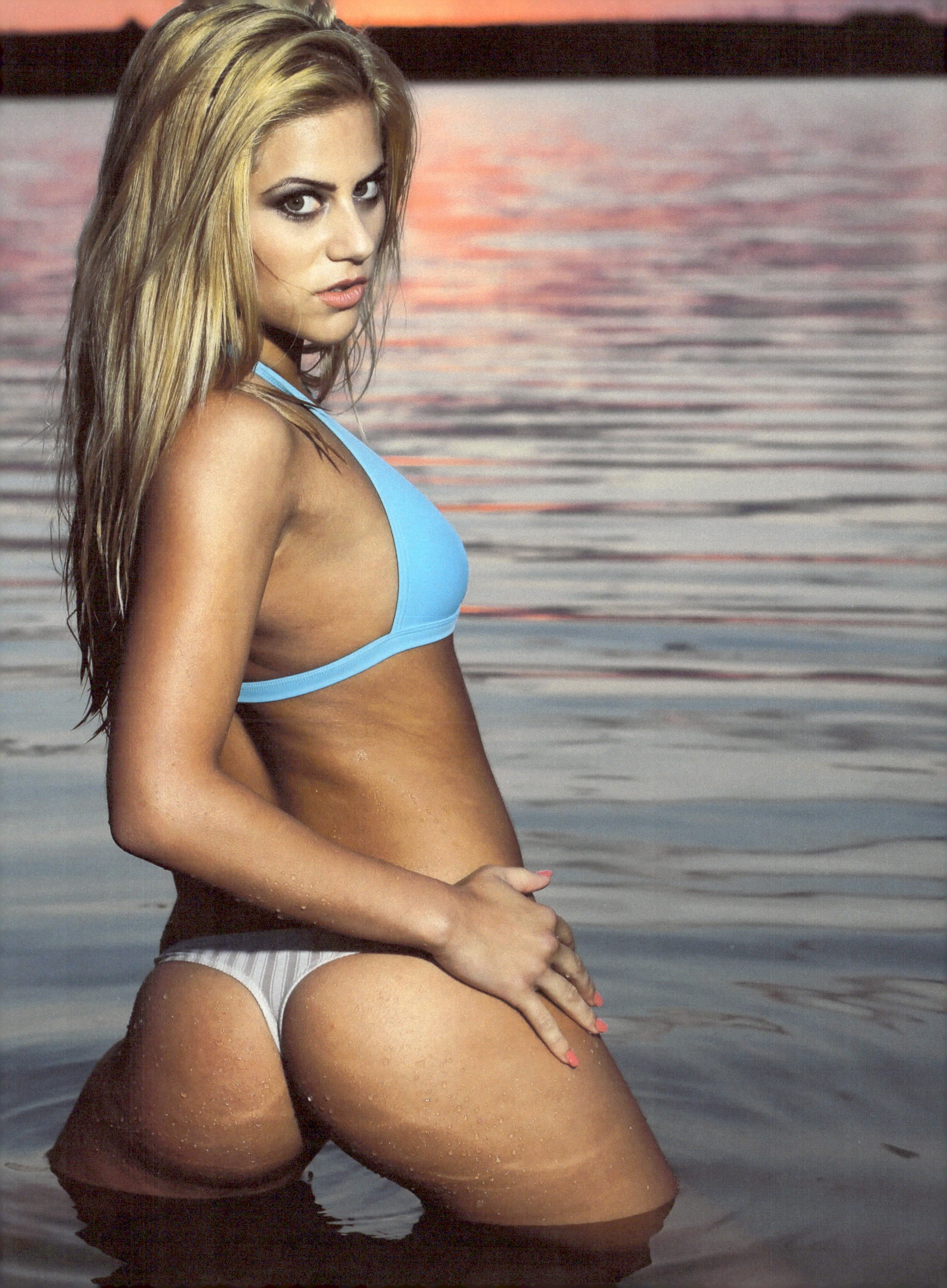

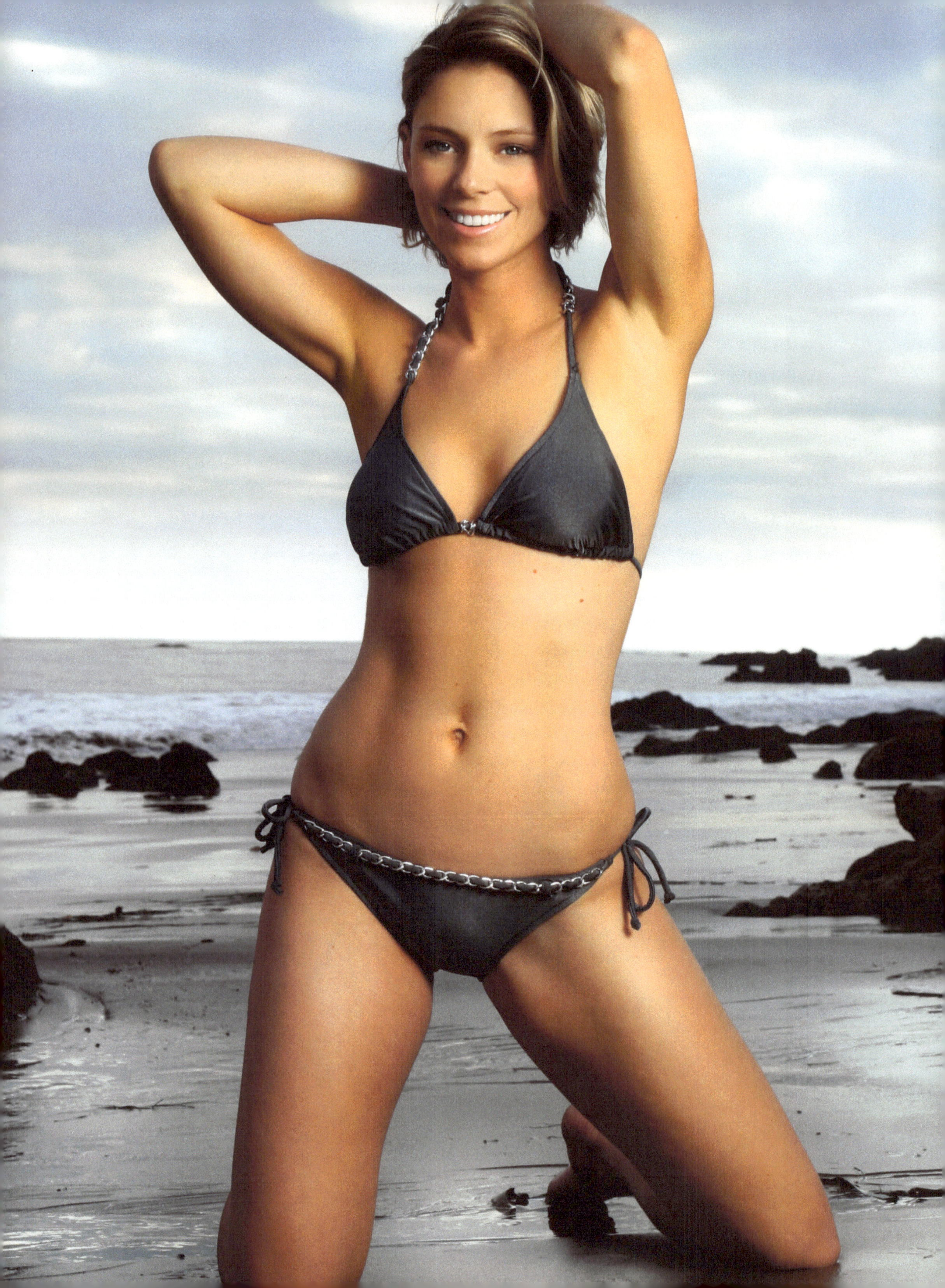

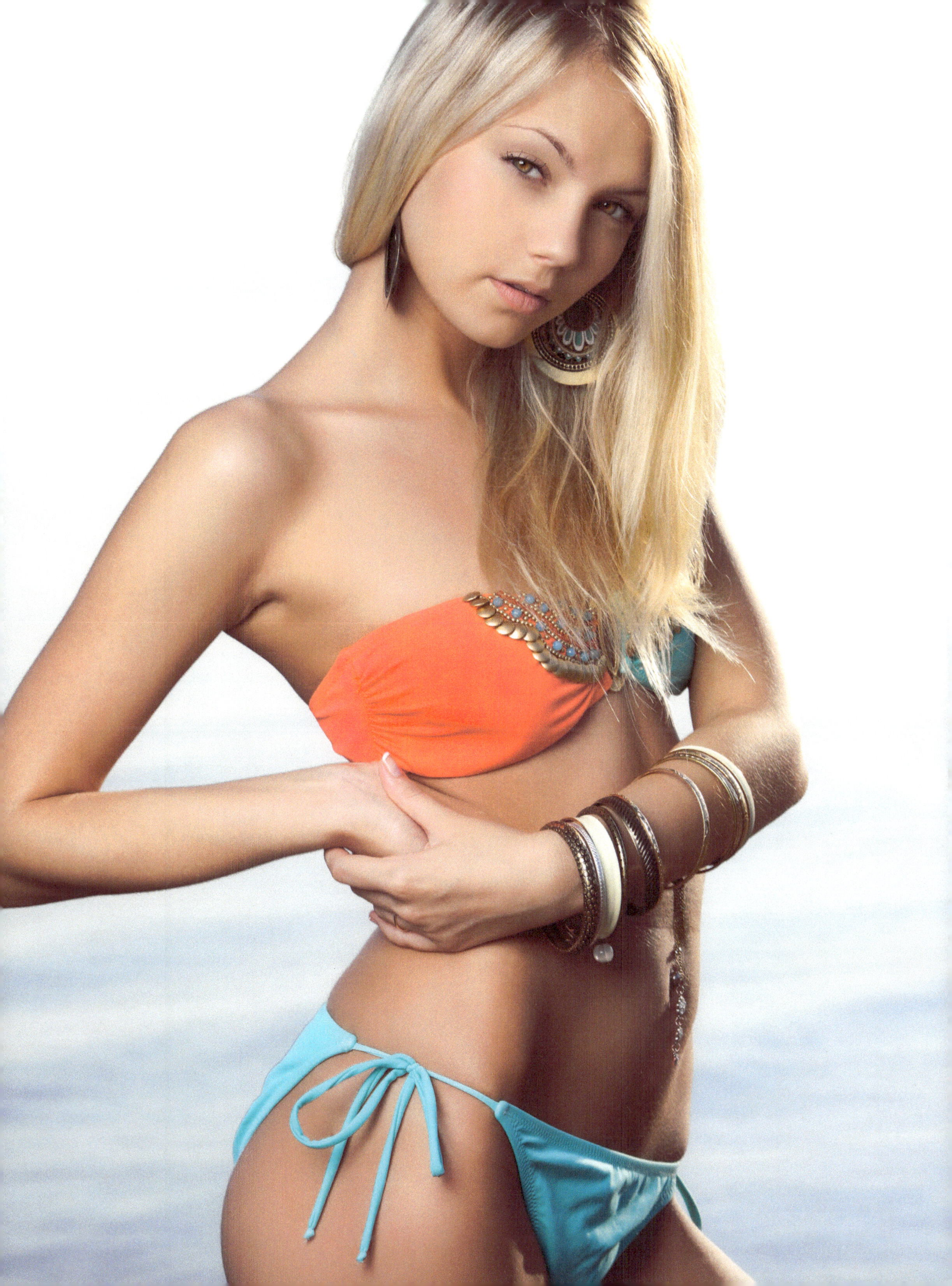

www.ingramcontent.com/pod-product-compliance
Lightning Source LLC
Chambersburg PA
CBHW050422180526
45159CB00005B/2370
* 9 7 8 1 5 3 9 6 2 6 8 7 9 *